Wildey: Sel
Poetry and
Paul D. Wildey

WILDEY: SELECTED POETRY AND PROSE

First edition. April 20, 2024.

ISBN: 979-8223500629

Written by Paul D. Wildey.

Table of Contents

Dedication

This collection is dedicated to everyone that has ever broken my heart, without whom I never would have learned to use words as glue.

Foreword: Reading Wildey
J.Tony Staples

I met Paul when he was not quite half my age, but that was long ago and he's catching up fast. What struck me at the start, and has stayed with me since, is his uncanny knack for saying the thing that cuts through the crap, hits the mark, and does it without pissing you off or putting you on the defensive. Somehow, he makes, "You're full of shit," sound like constructive criticism, not hacking on you, but cajoling you simply to get over yourself and jump back into the mosh pit.

That definitely comes across in, "Wildey: Selected Poetry and Prose." One tracks a life spent recognizing one's OWN self-defeating fuckery, seeking transcendence of self-delusion. Honest expressions of personal truth tend to resonate, because we are all more alike than different. And "Wildey" is certainly honest.

I set out with the posture of a critic, assessing the behaviors and attitudes described in his writing, making smug mental notes about this bit being naked and honest, while that bit seems a bit self-pitying, judging whether or not I would have said or done the same, etc., etc. A little way in, however, it occurred to me that I was able to do that because all of it is so well-expressed. The time spent choosing words and crafting phrases jumps off the page. Reading "Wildey" is a decent playbook for anyone who wants to take that notorious journey of self-discovery (dunt- dunt- DUUUUUH!!).

The fact that the short first piece reads like an epitaph sets us up perfectly. "Untitled" toppled my ancient bias against "rhymey" verse. The rhymes helped me hear someone going over the same reproaches and grievances all night. "I'm Sorry" intriguingly uses the title phrase as a bracket to talk about a different topic [spoiler alert]: sleep, leaving us to work out for ourselves the impulse to apologize. It's introspection time, fuckers.

Next, we have three compact prose pieces. "Dream" exemplifies Wildey's Bukowski influence, with startling jumps between the sublime and profane. "Fuck the Muse" is the prose equivalent of the jaded artist, tearing up their own work in a fit of self- condemnation. "On the Hook" is a textbook example of a wordsmith turning a metaphor into a conceit.

Full disclosure: I love "Daunt," the earliest poem in this collection. The alliterative runs and galloping wordplay belie a deeper metaphysics, reminiscent of Ginsberg. "Daunt" yearns for meaning, aches for a spiritual connection, stands in awe of the staring void.

As a Survivor of harsh codependent relationships, "Vampyr" hits close to home. It is hard to illumine the paradox of fascination with one's own predator. Paul does it with "Vampyr."

The chill of "Mid-December" is pristine from the first line to the last, and what follows it is nothing less than Shakespearean. The Bard had a genius for dropping a smidgen of comic relief into his tragedies, as a way of setting rhythm and tempo. After the horror-inspired "Mid-December," and the philosophical musings of "Soliloquy," and "Poet or Poem?" we get a "Roses are Red" offering that is so stupid it transcends mere genius. Hurray for weed!

"Blue" has the charm of Poe and Gorey, deftly blending the romantic and the macabre, the sweet and the creepy. As for "Coffee and Cream," the line, "Six pall-bearers taking out the trash," is the type of thing I point to when I say. "THIS! This, right here! This cat can write his ass off."

If you want to know the bitter irony of being loved by someone who wants to change you, look it up in "Dictionary."

"Letter Not Sent" reads like beat poetry, and that is my jam. The sense of being haunted by lost love again meets Wildey's passion for horror in "A Mournful Notion," artfully framing the beauty of the macabre. "This Moment" carries the same subtle pride in one's scars that I hear in "Veteran of a Thousand Psychic Wars."

I love a good haiku, and "Morning Haiku" is good, joyfully abandoning syntax and semantics and still communicating that one, focused feeling: moment captured.

"Dog Shit" is Bukowski meets Silverstein. That should be impossible. WTF, Paul? This is dope! "Inconsequential" also has a bot of that silly meets serious vibe, and the result is incredibly poignant. As long as I am name-dropping, "Love and Dying" easily rivals the tone of Reznor, with the unexpected hip-hop scent of Mos Def.

"Riverbank" is a bittersweet watercolor depiction of that sad, black and purple moment when you and your partner both realize it's over at the same time. This is cleverly followed by "Alone," reminding us that, no, it's never really over. Not really.

Finally, "Holiday Parade" escorts us to the egress. I fuckin love Bukowski, and I consistently get the same paradoxical ability to present ugliness in beautiful ways from Wildey's writing. This last piece exemplifies that, and throws in a bit of Kerouac and Burroughs for good measure.

The result: a completely unique and singular style that runs through "Wildey" like a strain of creepy chanting children on a Danny Elfman soundtrack. From pastoral to pissed off, from class to crass, "Wildey" will explain why great writers hope their kids don't become great writers. Blunt honesty is a rich sustained diet.

- - -

02-24-2024, Underbridge, Olywa

- - -

Regret

I have never regretted love
The regret lies in loss

Untitled

I wrote another poem for you
Not that you care to read it
Such praise and accolades
From others who have seen it
You're magic for my wordplay
Or maybe that's the pain
Even though you will ignore
It's better out of my brain

I wrote another poem for you
Such a sweet refrain
Reverberating through my head
Swirling down the drain
Words etched in my psyche
Now on this paper play
I don't know why I'm still at it
You'll always go away

I wrote another poem for you
In hopes to make you stay
Or maybe in hopes to quell my demons
The ones that I should slay
Beauty found in my dark corners
The ones all filled with dust
Beauty for someone else's eyes
Someone I shouldn't trust

I wrote another poem for you
Trying to forget my lust
A poem you may never see
Just ignore it if you must
I just want you to see
The love that lives in me
I just want to get it out
In hopes I will be free

I'm Sorry

I'm sorry.
I'm so fucking sorry.
All I've ever wanted was to be understood.
Experience and study taught me how unrealistic that was.
Over the years I found comfort in pain.
Alienation became an identity.
If no one could be there for me, the darkness always would be.
I've been ripped screaming from far too many peaceful slumbers to not romanticize the void.
I've read many quotes from people I admire, opining the waste of life that is sleep.
How my relationship with sleep is so different was confusing for so long.
Eventually, it became obvious that all I wanted was a break from the tortured wailing in my mind.
No one bothers you when you sleep.
No matter how much you've injured someone's dignity, no matter how many responsibilities you left aside only to grow to gargantuan obstacles, no matter how much someone thinks they need you...
No one bothers you when you sleep.
When you awaken to anguish, to a sickness in your gut, to a disease in your soul, it becomes a dreaded obligation.
All the peace I've ever known has come in those unconscious hours.
I want that to change.
I always have.
The mind, unlike the body, takes conscious effort to heal.
Rest is all that's needed to convalesce from a corporeal wound or affliction.

To heal the rifts in a fractured psyche, one must tear down the walls built to protect vulnerability.
Those walls are made of me.
Tearing them down hurts.
At times, the work to heal is more agonizing than a life lived under the agony of a past misused.
People have forged relationships with me.
Accepted me.
Attempted to aid in the progress toward a sound mind.
Compassion is terrifying.
Loss, alienation, and failure are risks implied in the undertaking of social intercourses.
The very things that make those relationships necessary are merely biding their time to double down when the generosity of our cohorts inevitably dries up.
Despite all efforts to the contrary, every moment spent forging connections, I found myself alone again every night, simply waiting for sleep to take me.
I regret my habits.
A life forged in routine.
Routine comprised of identifying with my torment.
Routine of retreating into darkness for fear of light.
Belief in the transient quality of human relationships led me to estrange those most invested in my well being.
Those that may never have left.
I'm doing the work.
I'm giving it the old college try.
I still just want to sleep.
I'm sorry.
I'm so fucking sorry.

Dream

For one blissful moment, I was whole. I was at peace. The world swirled around me in flashes of gold and green. I could hear your voice, sweet like honey, gently caressing my inner ear. All at once it was gone. I was in my recliner with half a beer spilt in my crotch.

There's a strange serenity that comes with knowing everything is still broken, and a sense of purpose brought on by stripping wet pants before entering the shower. I hope it washes away any notion that life is out there waiting. The longing need not plague my sleep again.

Fuck the Muse

You would think that when I am this deep in a pool of my own torment and the words are flowing out of me like greasy hangover shits that I would tuck in and labor towards the completion of another chapter or screenplay. Yet here I sit, loquaciously spilling my guts on Facebook. Why toil toward a fulfilling end? A piece of art worthy of consideration? I'd rather troll for emotional responses from those foolish enough to expect my social media to be an exercise in frivolity. Despite all claims to the contrary, I do not wax poetic in an effort to turn the grotesque corners of my life to beauty. I do so to appear to others as though I have control over the emotions that spoil my slumber. I do so in an attempt to reap admiration for my ability to explore and articulate the grievances I am left with in the dark of the night. There's no point in spelunking these deep caves of dismay if no one sees me do it. Give me likes, you fuckers. My gratification must be immediate.

On the hook

I'm on the hook like a side of beef. Kept in the cold, dark locker for fear of spoiling. My carcass yields potential bounty, coveted by those in need and yet, you hold me here. You won't partake yourself, turning instead to the aging and potentially diseased meat, rotting in your fridge.

I'm on the hook like a side of beef. Kept in the cold, dark locker for fear of spoiling. Who knows when you will want my New York strip. My tenderloin. All begging to be seasoned and attended to. Oh, what delights await you if you just choose to care enough to utilize them

I'm on the hook like a side of beef. Kept in the cold, dark locker for fear of spoiling. The hard part is already done. You've gutted me. Removed the undesired organs and left only glistening possibilities. You need not want for I already belong to you. Bought, paid for, and carefully butchered.

I'm on the hook like a side of beef. Kept in the cold, dark locker for fear of spoiling. I could have been purchased by a restaurant and fed a mass of eager mouths. I could have been appreciated by so many lovers sharing my bounty. Yet here I hang. On the hook. In the dark. Greedily held for fear of spoiling.

Daunt

I am the reflection of pain, devine.
I mark occasions with incantations, quotations, and innovations.

The canid ravenous rebuttals of full-on fantastical studies, weighs on my sullied shoulders.

Can I escape the linguistic follies of fortified fortuitous break-downs?

I am alone in this chase. Running an unorchestrated race.
Am I the mouthful of spunky breeder-seeds swimming ever closer to the digestive tract of the world? Pushing potent, potential productivity to the cancerous colon of hell?
These inquiries are uttered into the nothing. Falling with tremendous clatter upon the echoing caverns of deaf ears.

Trying, struggling, ferociously fighting... I can't save you.

Dog paddling dangerous distances, toward dancing depths, of decaying deceit. Death looms.

Blood clots of the brain-stem bloom into bountiful, botanical, bouquets, of brilliant, bandstanding.

Can we understand underestimated utilitarian utterances?

Never again shall negative negotiations negate navigable nether-regions of necrotic neurosis.

Fountains of foreskin fascinations, form follies of fornications founded in flippant fantasies.

Creeping along narrow precipices, on the ravine of self-deception and radical actualization.

Find me beneath the willows, grass as my pillow, lying on the earth, as I will one day do within it.

You cannot stop the tic-toc of of mortality's clock.

My own lustful libido pushes me closer to the arms of another introverted, introspective, interloper. Perverted in potential piousness.

The shadows exist of the light, the light of the void's antithesis.

Where is the yin to my yang? The rama-lama to my ding-dong? The prose to my sing-song?

Balance is desired and never acquired. Striving for the ethereal reality that guides and drives. Rapidly ascending the Bell Curve of the human experience.

The other side is just as steep.

Success is descent.

Joy and ambition test the testers.

Who keeps tally on the universal scoreboard in the sky? Is it even a game? Sometimes, savage sentience sentences saviors to silent sovereign soundscapes. Sometimes, to death.

Ambling forward to the amicable heights of ecstatic questions. Who are we? Why are we? Will time lead to unity, conformity, deformity, or reformed rampages of radiant repercussions?

These answers are not for the worldly. Not for the sentient.

To understand is to transcend the rigid thought processes of incumbent reality.
Speaking without vocal chords to the spiritual divinity within us all.

Make it stop.

Keep it going.

Consciousness destroys free-form organic growth. Development at the hands of man marks the destruction of nature's own designs.

Another flight through clouds of cohesive conversations attempting to conserve coital corrections. Natal naggings inside the bloated womb of interaction.

Before you all the possibilities of a broken world.

We have been blessed with tools, now crumbling in their disregard.

Towing trembling transitions across the plains of progress. What can be done, and what will, seldom reside in respectful realms.

To find your aligned axiom of analytical approach, rely on readily ratified rantings.

The world is your oyster. Satisfy your appetite. The pollution strengthens the immunity.

Vampyr

I felt my blood drain from my neck the first time you kissed it. I ignored it, because the thought of giving you life was so enticing that you taking mine in the process never occurred to me. Love is always giving, without question. However, those deserving of love do so in return. I was so focused on holding you that I never realized I was also carrying my own weight.

How quickly you let go makes me think you never wanted me to begin with, but you begging for the door to be left open only proves the fangs in your mouth. I mistook the hunger in your eyes for love. You have the thirst. It was bestowed upon you.

I've always been far too ready to bleed. What a hapless scenario. I don't even know if you're aware of what you've become. If you know your own need to destroy. But destroy you have, and I have revoked your invitation. You have no power here. My blood is my own. I hope your coffin is cold. There's no cure for this disease, but death. My only wish for you is that the steak comes quickly.

Mid-December

I feigned bravery as the trees whispered of demise
As the moon shown ghosts through the clouds in the sky
My breath blew cold around my cigarette's ember
That fateful night in mid-December

I saw her through a standing grove
Caught the scent of incense; myrrh, and clove
A pallid witch stood gaunt and ghastly
As the forest yawned and stretched so vastly

She strode ominously, though not really striding
Moving forward, with a foreboding gliding
Her hand outstretched, gnarled and twisted
Fingers twitching as she shuddered and shifted

My blood ran cold as the crone then spoke
A terror inside me shuddered and woke
A snapping of twigs or a breaking of bones
Rang in her call as she stood there alone

"What brought to my wood such a foolish young man?
What stops me from killing you right where you stand?
What stops me from rending your pitiful soul?
You came here to die, though that not be your goal."

My feet were planted as though cast in cement.

19

My heart in my throat as I wished she'd relent
Closer she grew as my hair did stand
Why was I indeed in this forsaken land?

I had no god to which I could beg for forgiveness
What chance did I stand against this treacherous business?
Surely I didn't deserve to fall at my unripened young age
I gazed in her eyes, her face twisted in rage

"Please set aside my careless trespassing
For the losses I suffer continue amassing
Despite my melancholy and my musings of death
I am not ready to forego my trembling breath."

The ghoul was now close, her hand still outstretched
The incense replaced by a foul rotting stench
She gazed deeply into my watering eyes
My terror dampened what would have been cries

She declared again in a cackling croak
The sound and the stench made me wretch and then choke
"Your losses amass as your heart has grown black
Your trespasses prove that there is no turning back"

Her grizzly hand plunged deep in my chest
Grasping firmly the pump that beat in my breast.
My shirt became sticky and glistening with blood
As my life drained forth and pooled in the mud

I knew she was right, I was now too far gone
Calloused and jaded for ever so long

I came to appreciate her need to dismember
That fateful night in mid-December

Soliloquy

Cathartic soliloquies clatter against the barren walls of my domicile. Bereft of anyone to share with, I confide in the void. Syllables contrived of suffering and study, their elegance belongs to me, and now to the vacuous spaces that largely comprise my studio. I feel empty, yet I am able to pour forth an abundance. Like a pitcher of tea at a picnic. Filling the nothing without me with sweetly serenading confessions. From the cup that is this echo chamber I drink in my own musings. Filling myself with certainty I knew not that I had to offer. The cold air swirls with a release of purposeful breath, the reverberation of which serves to occupy my cavernous head. What once was empty now is full and it is all for nothing. Everything for no one.. save myself and my walls.

Poet or Poem?

Am I a poet, or am I a poem?

Am I composing this glorious mess, or is this catastrophe composing me?

Do I take the madness and turn it to beauty, or is the exquisiteness rending my sanity?

Is each piece of art an accomplishment in it and of itself, or yet another line in the epic that shall be concluded upon death?

Am I writing about you, or are you writing yourself upon my existence?

Is the struggle with the unfinished page, or am I struggling to accept that so many years lay yet to be composed?

A Poem in Four Lines

Roses are red
Your ass is fantastic
I'm so high right now
My eyes feel like plastic

Blue

If you're contagious
Please infect me
Let me die from your disease
I want to drown
In the pools of your eyes
Hold me under please

You're aching joints
Anxious stomach
Your begging pleas
Even so tortured
Your voice so sweet
I disappear with ease

If you're dying
Take my breath
And stay another day
I want to suffocate
In your embrace
And never go away

Your gentle touch
Your coldest shoulder
The wants that you convey
Myself alone here
Yourself a prop

PAUL D. WILDEY

Life is but a play

If you're sleepless
Please just wake me
I want to hear your thoughts
I want to wander
Aimless and free
Through your forget-me-nots.

Coffee and Cream

There are people here who want me dead
And only some of them are in my head
Steady diet on non fasting days
Rare illusions and straight malaise

I never cared much for fancy cars
I used to go broke going out to bars
I met you in a movie scene
A pretty nightmare, coffee and cream

It's not so sweet when you love another
Silent assassin undercover
Wake up screaming reaching out for guns
Inside my mind seven burning suns

I'm late for everything it all can wait
Wish I was late now, body and wake
Six pallbearers taking out the trash
Another bottle and the glass I smash

I'm just a cog that hates machines
Drunk and smoking all the lies and things
Another rift set in a dream
Another nightmare coffee and cream

It's not so sweet when you love another

Silent assassin undercover
Wake up screaming reaching out for guns
Inside my mind seven dying suns

I fell apart and you held me close
Mutated mindset microdose
Illusions spring and hearts they break
Into black lungs the breaths we take

Never asked to be a millionaire
Would rather just not gasp for air
Walking on glass with feet of steam
Decaying nightmare coffee and cream

It's not so sweet when you love another
Silent assassin undercover
Wake up screaming reaching out for guns
Inside my mind seven burning suns

Dictionary

Why read the dictionary if you have nothing to say?
Does it even count if you never say it?
I know I'm so much more than this, but you're always disappointed, married to potential.

I fell in love with all the things you are.
All the things I am coalesce in a pool of beautiful possibilities.
So many ideas.
So many abilities.
So many opportunities.
All the best players on one team.
Never won a game.
A fortune means nothing never spent.
Tears have more purpose seldom wept.
And yet...

All the things I still could be
A mind and time commingled free
The art is in me, so better out
But it's all for me without a doubt.

All the things you are, I know. A book read until the pages tatter. I'd offer you a movie deal if I were a producer, but you're not an author and filmmaking is another facet of my life unrealized.

I know you look upon me as a lump of clay. Yourself kiln-fired to permanence.
So much stability.
So much form.
So much steadfastness.
All the best engineers on one project.
Finished in record time.
A forest means nothing never explored.
Years have more purpose with few more.
And yet...

All the things you chose to be,
Not one of them for the sake of me.
I try to form the best I can,
But you love potential and not a man.

Letter Not Sent

I just wrote another letter I will never send. Locked in the box of lovelorn communiques too self indulgent to besmirch the eyes of their subject. More blood shed on a page in a ritualistic attempt to sate the demons banging at the doors of my mind. The poetic cadence of desire enriched by the luscious weight of dysphoria. I find myself wanting to disappear into the pages, to dance in the ashes of razed romance, to wallow in the shallow and stagnant water of hope held out of spite. Nights like this I can't stop writing. The bliss of release cheapened ever so subtly by the knowledge that no matter the beauty of my verbiage, no turn of phrase will ever truly dull the pain. One more cocktail, and a half-hearted affirmation directed toward growth. Three more hours in front of the keyboard. I'll cry myself to sleep once tugging the strings of my anguish fails to elicit the desired chemical response.

A Mournful Notion

I have still not come to believe that I will never lay eyes upon you again. So many years and so many miles are not the only things that separate us. For mortality has its filthy fingers around your neck. Your visage came in a dream. Reminding me of long abandoned hope. Your rose colored cheeks now ashen and your emerald eyes tarnished and greyed. Your voice trembled under the weight of the news you bestowed upon me. Few precious minutes were now your only worldly possession.

I pleaded, I wept, I prayed to awaken. I yearned for one last caress of your fingertips, though I knew they held no warmth. I confessed my heart had broken the day I left you behind. You replied in kind. Your claim that unhealed wounds had led us to this meeting made me retch. I beseeched your ghostly presence forgiveness. Forgiveness that never came.

I reached for you as you faded away. Your woeful words morphing into the wailing of my phone. As I saw the moniker on the screen I felt the blood drain from my face. What reason would your father have to contact me after all these tortured years, had your visit been a product of my unconscious mind?

My funeral suit would need to be cleaned. I would need to steel myself against the geering eyes of your loved ones. I already knew my whiskey breath would waft through a wake like the sound of an insincere apology.

The ringing ceased and a deafening silence fell over my room. The room that I wished were a tomb. How had I come so far as to believe I had forgotten you. To believe I could soldier on in a world without you in it. Bereft of your embrace I found solace in knowing that you had found peace. A mournful notion knowing what I know now.

In a post-apocalyptic head space I stumbled to the bathroom, across acres of anguish. After splashing my face in the sink, I found myself staring into the eyes of a broken man. Just behind however I saw the face of my beloved. I turned to face you, but a door of mahogany stood in your stead. I swear I heard your airy whisper grace my ear. Tidings of a will I seldom believe myself to possess. A will to go on. If you only knew, you wouldn't ask this of me.

Collapsed on the floor, I buried my face in my hands. I began to chuckle at first, before bursting forth with maniacal laughter. How had it just occurred to me? This blessing of your presence? For so long you were so far away, and I now felt you more in a few fleeting moments than I had ever believed I would again. Despite what fate may have done to your corporeal being, you were mine again. In death you were mine alone.

No one could ever take you away again.

This Moment

There are one thousand failures of my past waging bloody war with one thousand possibilities of my future on the battlefield that is this exact moment. A moment in which I could be completely and utterly at peace if it were not for the incessant distraction of battling abstractions.

Morning Haiku

Rat's nest head fog groan
Coffee burble smoking choke
Libido crisis

Dog Shit

The grass isn't greener
It's covered in dog shit
Nobody's happy
We're all just fakin' it
One more hit
Maybe we'll make it through
Two more drinks
Maybe I'll feel like you
Happy birthday
Wishing for death day
Thirty more years
There's no fucking way
Stale body odor
From a hard days work
Another TV dinner
On a plastic fork
Holy shit, what a life
Wasted on cocaine
Cheap whiskey, marijuana
Do I even have a brain?
Can I feel anything but pain?
Who else is insane?
Every day is the same
This dog shit's fucking lame

.

Inconsequential

Tossing his cigarettes on the table, he watched them bounce, roll, and topple to the floor. Another trivial yet, mysteriously hard-hitting failure. He picked them up and tossed them again. They ricocheted off the corner of the table landing mockingly at his feet. He chuckled. He might have wept.

Love and Dying.

Your voice is a symphony. Your absence is a cacophony. Your eyes are a portal. This phone makes me mortal. Three hours alone, I want to be home. Home is in your arms. Honesty is harm.

I look to days of ignorance for bliss. I look to tomorrow and wish for more of this. Once deceived, now relieved. Our love conceived, I had believed.

Fortunate for fast fornication. Sucker for synthesized salvation. Maladjusted motivation. Unproductive provocation.

One time for the pain in me. The damaged brain in me. The light insane in me. You have free reign on me.

Forget it. Regret it. Remember resonance. Disremember innocence.

Dump truck me. Fist fuck me.

Let me weep. Let me sleep.

Forget me nots. Pitch black thoughts.

I can't move. Try to improve. Sadistic groove. Nothing to prove.

I am alone. Take me home.

Riverbank

Hand in hand by the riverbank
We pondered its fleeting nature
We never once considered
That we had the same feature

Hand in hand by the riverbank
We considered its raw power
The connection between us
Raging past by the hour

Hand in hand by the riverbank
We observed it coursing free
We knew in that moment
It would never be you and me

Hand in hand by the riverbank
We watched the rapids swell
Our hands, they came apart
I think it's just as well

Alone

Every night alone
Steals a piece of my soul
Each one a night
I could have spent with you
You who stole
A piece of my tired heart
You who stole
My will to sleep alone

Holiday Parade

With your voice still echoing in my ears and your visage still reflected in negative when I close my eyes my phone brings tidings of your oblivious hold on who you are to me. Crisp bubbles tickle my throat as ethanol burns my nose hairs. My melancholy art pales in comparison to the post-punk melodies drenching me from the other side of the bar. I feel disgusted in myself, like I just opened my pants for a piss only to take in the stench of a three day old hockey game. This is the sweat of the soul, however. Scribbling desperately in an attempt to force sense out of disorder. Meter never comes. My fervent scrambling toward organizing this malcontent, met by even more free form feelings. Grinding as hard as my arms will let me push, I must loosen my grip for friends and foes joining the holiday parade from the door to oblivion. I lean in, begging for resolve, but find my knuckles bit by the grinder or my eyes tinged by the sparks. No matter my resolve, I see these words may never truly hone to a cutting edge. It matters not, for I know not what they were meant to cut to begin with.

About the Author

Paul Wildey, a multi-faceted artist and storyteller, finds inspiration in the eerie landscapes of the Pacific Northwest and the haunting realms of horror. At 35, Wildey has woven a collection of poetry and prose that delves into the depths of human emotion, often drawing parallels to the macabre and the enigmatic. Initially hailing from Olympia, WA, Wildey currently calls Spanish Fork, Utah, home.

Wildey's artistic journey spans various creative mediums - from writing and directing short horror films to lending his voice and lyricism to diverse musical projects. His exploration of drawing, painting, sculpture, and photography adds layers of visual storytelling to his portfolio. Moreover, his earlier contributions as a writer for an online magazine covering underground music in the Pacific Northwest offer a testament to his devotion to artistic expression and community engagement.

Forged by the immortal works of literary maestros such as Edgar Allan Poe and Charles Bukowski, as well as the poetic legacy of early beat poets like Ginsberg, Wildey's writing bears the indelible mark of these influences. His deep-seated passion for the horror genre is evident in his expansive collection of over 400 films, serving as a wellspring of inspiration for his dark and compelling narratives.

As an artist who thrives on delving into the shadows and unraveling the mysteries that lie within, Paul Wildey invites readers on a captivating journey through his evocative and diverse body of work. His creative odyssey continues to resonate with those who seek the beauty and terror that lurk within the human experience.

Milton Keynes UK
Ingram Content Group UK Ltd.
UKHW020941220424
441551UK00019B/1491